Bicycle Touring with Children
A Guide to Getting Started

Nancy Sathre-Vogel

www.familyonbikes.org

Bicycle Touring with Children

A Guide to Getting Started

Published in the United States by:

Old Stone Publishing

ISBN 978-0-9837187-1-0

Table of Contents

Who Am I and Why Am I Writing This Book?

We were just your ordinary, everyday, American family one day. The next we were anything but. In the spring of 2006 the four of us were living in a typical suburban American home in Boise, Idaho.

The boys attended second grade at a local elementary school and played on soccer teams and swam with swim teams. I taught Special Ed at a local middle school and played with beads in the evenings. My husband taught science at the same school. In short – life was typical and predictable.

But a couple months later, the four of us were living a life very few can imagine. We arose every morning in our tent, packed our sleeping bags, strapped all our earthly belongings onto our bicycles, and pedaled away to face the adventures of the day – of which there were plenty!

How did that transformation happen?

I suppose I could give some trite answer here– we woke up one day and decided we wanted more… yadda, yadda, yadda… But the reality is that I honestly don't know how it all came to be.

What I do know is that I've always been adventurous and independent and (perhaps) a little foolhardy. My mom told me stories of when I was little – of how I scared the pants off her with my antics. And I know that my wanderlust began in earnest when my parents took me to Mexico when I was sixteen – my eyes were opened to the fact that there was a whole world out there!

I'm sure my time in the Peace Corps in Honduras helped push me along, as did the two years I taught in Egypt with my husband. We spent a year cycling the Indian subcontinent and our Christmas and summer vacations found us pedaling in various parts of the world. During our seven years in Ethiopia our twin boys were born, and they moved with us to Taiwan and then on to Malaysia.

So by the time we moved to my hometown of Boise, Idaho when the boys were seven, we had been around the world a time or two. We had also learned to thrive on the unexpected nature of travel in third world nations.

But yet – there was another side of us. That side that believed – truly believed – that to be a "proper" parent, one must do what's expected. One must drop the kids off at daycare, work all day, pick the kids up, fix a quick dinner, take the kids to soccer practice, and then collapse into bed utterly exhausted. After all – that's what society raised us to believe is right. That's what we should want.

And so it was that I went about my daily routine. I taught all day dealing with unruly teenagers. By the time I got home, I was too tired to truly enjoy my own boys. But I didn't question it because…well, I was living the American Dream – and doesn't everybody want the American Dream?

And then came the day – that beautiful spring day in March of 2006. That day, my husband slumped into our house after a particularly rough day in the classroom and collapsed into his favorite chair by the window. His eyes glazed over and I knew he wasn't looking at the lawn which desperately needed mowing or the barn which needed fixing. He was farther away. Much farther away.

"Nancy," he said. "I'm tired of this. Every day I get up and go to school and spend all day with other people's kids. I want time with Davy and Daryl – time to watch them grow and see them learn. I want to buy a triple bike and head out with the boys. Let's do it, Nancy. Let's quit our jobs and head out."

I started thinking about our life in Boise, Idaho and the American Dream? And I started to wonder about the real question: Was this the way I wanted it to be? Was the American Dream the be-all and end-all? Was it the path to enlightenment and roadway to happiness? Would I, *could I*, be content with a big house in the suburbs and some cars? Was that really what life was all about?

Within a few weeks we had made the decision to go for it. Life was too short not to and besides – our boys would never be eight years old again. Two months later we headed out to see our country with our boys.

We spent one year on the road that time. Twelve months of being together, growing together, learning together. 365 days of taking on challenges together as a family and triumphing over them. In short – it was one year of magic.

After that the decision to take off again came easily. We knew the challenges we would face. We knew the rewards. We knew the magic.

A year later we began a 17,000-mile trek from Alaska to Argentina. We reached the southern end of the world after nearly three years on the road. In all we camped on the side of the road about 800 nights, and consumed more granola bars than I can count. We also grew together as a family and forged a bond that cannot be broken. And for us – that's what keeps us going.

I've grown to love this family bike touring lifestyle and want others to discover the joy I've found. Whether you plan to hit the road for a long weekend to Grandma's house or pedal around the world with your children, you'll find valuable information here which will help you along.

Chapter 1: Can I Tour with my Children?

People ask me for advice all the time – how can they take a bicycle trip with their kids? What little tidbits of information can I pass on to help them plan their own family cycling adventure in various parts of the world? I think they expect me to say something like, "Take your child out cycling regularly to build up his strength," or "Make sure the bike and cycling clothes fit properly."

But honestly, **the best bit of advice I can give is to never doubt your child**. Never, ever doubt your child – not even for one nanosecond.

You see, **children have this uncanny ability to live up to their parents' expectations**. Somehow, kids know exactly what their parents expect them to do – and they do exactly that. If parents expect their children to pedal around the block, they'll do it!! And if parents expect their children to cycle around the world, they'll do that too. **It's us – as parents – who tend to limit our children.**

We are the ones who look at our kids and say, "You're just a kid. You can't do that!" But do we ever ask our kids what they can do? Rarely. We tend to assume they can't do it – and so they can't. Or maybe we assume they won't do it – so they won't.

I remember way back when I taught first grade for the first time. I had always taught older kids and had no idea what first graders could or could not do. My school had no curriculum to guide me, and very little in the way of books – so I made my own way through that first year. It was a challenge in many ways, but I just modified what I had done with my older kids and did that with my younger ones.

I taught my six-year-olds all about atoms and molecules that year. They became protons and neutrons crammed into a nucleus or electrons spinning around it and they made models of atoms using Styrofoam balls for the particles.

Once my kids understood all about molecules we moved on to surface tension and density and air pressure and all kinds of complicated scientific concepts. It never occurred to me that my students couldn't learn it all – so they did. Each and every one of those little guys went home at night and explained to their parents all about how the polarity in a water molecule caused surface tension – and how we could weaken that tension by putting soap on it.

Then I went to university to work on my master's degree, and talked with many other first grade teachers. "You teach your kids that?" they asked. "First graders aren't capable of learning that!"

And you know what? I have no doubt whatsoever that their first graders weren't capable of learning it – because they weren't expected to. In retrospect, I'm glad I didn't know six-year-olds couldn't learn all those advanced scientific concepts - because I had a blast teaching it to them!

Taking kids on a bike tour is exactly the same – simply expect them to do it, and they will. Expect them to go out and have the time of their life and love the freedom and opportunities a bike tour gives them – and they will. They'll thrive on the opportunity to explore and discover the wonders of nature on their own. Kids can do a lot more than we give them credit for, but we have to allow them to do it – by believing in them.

Mark Twain once said, *"Twenty years from now you will be more disappointed by the things that you didn't do than by the ones you did do. So throw off the bowlines. Sail away from the safe harbor. Catch the trade winds in your sails. Explore. Dream. Discover."*

Tips for Getting Started

Start early: Don't wait until your child is a teenager before heading out on the bike. Kids learn to love what they grow up with, so make sure they are exposed to it from an early age.

Get the kids involved: Let your child know what's coming and encourage him to be involved in the planning. You will always have the final say, but try to incorporate your child's wishes in some manner.

Modify your schedule: Know from the outset that your pace will be different. Don't expect children to be able to handle the same level of physical demands you can.

Focus on making memories: Shift the focus from the destination to the process of getting there. Take the attitude that actually making it all the way around the world isn't as important as the time together as a family.

Chapter 2: Why Go Now?

If I had a penny for every time someone told me they hoped to head out to bike across the country once their kids have left home, I would be a rich woman. I've been stunned at how many people feel they need to stay home for 18 years until their kids are in college before taking off. I say: **go now**. Take advantage of every moment you have with your children before it is too late.

One day in 2006, shortly before we headed out for our first major family bicycle tour, I visited a friend of mine whose son had just committed suicide. Clinging to me as tears streamed down her face she said, **"Take advantage of every second you have with your boys. Don't wait until tomorrow. Tomorrow may never come."**

I was struck by those words. "Tomorrow may never come." Through her grief and torment, she uttered some of the wisest words I've ever heard, and I've thought about her words a lot in the hours we've spent pedaling the highways and byways together as a family.

There are many, many reasons to head out on a bicycle tour with your children – whether for an overnight trip to Grandma's house or a multi-year world tour.

Work together as a family toward a common goal:
In today's society, families aren't generally united in their efforts. Kids head off in the morning to their respective schools and parents are off to their jobs in different parts of the city. By the time everyone gets home at night, they are exhausted and still need to get homework done, dinner cooked, laundry washed, and the house cleaned. Work toward a common goal? You gotta be kidding me!

When on a bike tour, **each member of the family becomes part of the team.** Whether you are riding together on a tandem or each person rides her own single, you'll be working together to arrive at your destination. You'll find yourselves encouraging one another to get up the tough hills during the day, working together to get camp set up in the evening, and hanging out around the campfire at night. It's one of those rare opportunities to come together as a family without all the distractions of normal life.

Working together as a family to solve problems and overcome challenges will create an enduring bond between you and your children. You'll celebrate triumphs and suffer through adversity together, which can't help but change your relationship with your children.

Be a team:
On a bike tour, you will find you won't be parents and children, adults and kids, teachers and students – you'll be **equal members of a team.** Each member of the team comes in with certain strengths and weaknesses and you'll quickly figure out how to utilize each other's strengths to overcome their weaknesses.

Educational opportunities: On any bike tour, you will find many, many educational opportunities to take advantage of. Whether you are simply out for a weekend before the kids go back to school or are roadschooling your children on an extended tour, **the journey will help your children learn more about the world they live in.**

When you take a break in the desert, point out how the plants are specially designed for the dry, arid conditions. When you pass roadside historical signs, stop and read them together. Talk about how the movement of tectonic plates created the mountains you are cycling through. When it's raining discuss the water cycle.

Beyond "school": In addition to the many "school" subjects your child will learn on the road, she will learn about life itself from the bike. When she crests her first pass and gazes down upon the vast valley spread out below her, she'll learn the value of persistence. **Determination, stick-to-it-iveness, and understanding the thrill of victory are all very real benefits of a bike tour.**

Set an example: Parents are children's primary teacher. What kind of teacher do you want to be? By heading out on a bike tour with your children, you are **showing them that an active lifestyle is a rich, fulfilling way to live.** You are teaching your kids there is more to life than work, work, and more work.

Unplugged: With our dependence on electronic forms of entertainment, "unplugging" ourselves for a few days is a good thing. **Children learn to depend on Mother Nature for toys and know that electricity and batteries are not essential.**

Chapter 3: Choose the Right Bike(s)

Now more than ever, there is an amazing array of options available for family travel on bicycles. Each family will need to choose the right combination for their own personal circumstances. Consider your choice carefully.

Young Children

For children under about six years old, you will mostly likely have them attached to your bike in some manner. You've got many options to consider:

Trailer: Many families opt for a trailer for their young children. A trailer is wonderful in that the child can sleep when he wants, can play with toys while you are riding, and can be easily protected from the elements. In addition, the trailer may provide additional space for gear.

There are some disadvantages to the trailer, however. As your children rest in the comfort of the trailer, they will most likely sleep a good portion of the day – and then want to play all night when you need to sleep. Also, your children will not be actively working and helping to propel you along. For some children, this leads to frustration.

Tag-along: A tag-along (trailer bike, trail-a-bike) is a one-wheeled contraption that attaches to the back of your bike. On a tag-along your child will be able to pedal when he feels like it and rest when he wants.

Some tag-alongs come with gears, which are highly recommended so your child can help pedal up hills. This option has the advantage in that the child feels he is helping with the workload. When you reach the top of a hill, he knows he's helped and can be proud of his accomplishments. He is a member of a team and takes full credit for victories won.

Tag-alongs come in both a single-gear and multi-gear variety. If you want your child to be able to help at all on hills, get the one with gears.

The down side to the tag-along option is that the child is exposed to the elements and is not easily protected. Even with proper rain gear, it will be hard to keep his hands and feet warm and dry if the weather turns bad.

You've also got the issue of falling asleep on the bike. When he falls asleep, he will lean to the side throwing off the balance of your bike. Depending on traffic conditions at the time, this could lead to a dangerous situation.

In addition, energy is lost in every connection, so the tag-along is not as efficient as a tandem.

Tandem (or bigger multiple): Many of the advantages of the tandem are the same as for the tag-along – being part of a team and being able to help out with the workload.

The tandem also has the advantage of pedaling in sync. As the pedals are hooked together, a child on the back of a tandem learns to pedal with a normal cadence and is more closely connected to the captain. You can carry on a conversation easier due to sheer proximity. In addition, the tandem is more rigid than a tag-along so is a more efficient machine.

There are "kiddie cranks" available for tandems, which raise the pedals up to your child's feet. This is a great add-on as you can buy a bigger tandem and your child will have plenty of years of use from it. If the tandem is just slightly too big, pedal blocks can raise the pedals a couple of inches and are much easier than the kiddie crank.

Disadvantages of the tandem are primarily price related. Tandems are not cheap. Besides that, the tandem is forever together and you cannot simply disconnect it to run errands by yourself.

Another disadvantage to tandems or bigger multiples is the hassle of shipping them – they are very much oversized and some airlines won't take them. If you plan to travel with your multiple much, it is worth the extra money for S & S couplings so it can be dismantled into several, manageably-sized pieces.

Kids' Bike with Connector Coupling: Another option
that works for bike touring with kids is a coupler that connects an adult's bike to a small kid's bike. The child can ride his bike on his own when desired, but when tired or in heavy traffic can be towed behind Mom or Dad.

At the time of this writing, there were two couplers available: The Trail Gator tow bar and the Follow Me coupler. Although I've never used one of these devices personally, I've heard good reports from parents who have. They have the same advantages as the tag-along, but have the additional advantage of your child being able to ride solo part of the time.

The main disadvantage of the Trail Gator is that the rear of the bike is taken up by the coupler, which means less availability of space for gear. I've also heard reports that the Trail Gator may not be stable enough for long-term usage. I know of one family who used the FollowMe for thousands of miles and were happy with it.

Combinations: Many families have kids of varying ages, so find
a combination of some sort works best for them. A tandem with a trailer works well, and the tag-along companies are now making them so a trailer can be attached behind. It makes a long train, but allows a family to get out on tour – which is a good thing!

Older Children

When your child is a bit older, you've got other options and considerations to look at. Each child is different and has different capabilities. Consider your child!

Tag-along: A trailer bike is an option for short tours, but is not recommended for a longer tour with an older child. Due to the weight of the child, you would be putting a lot of stress on the connection system and on your bike – which could lead to damage. Even though they have improved the connection system, a trailer bike can never be as rigid as a tandem and therefore will never be as efficient as one. If the child is truly going to help pedal, get a tandem.

Tandem (or larger multiple): Tandems are a great option for older kids. Your child is still connected to you and you are in charge of maneuvering safely through traffic, but he is contributing to the workload and is a part of the team.

One downside to this option is the limited carrying space. You'll need to carry gear for two (or more) on only one bike. Another is the price issue – tandems don't come cheap and you can not convert it to a single bike for running errands. Also consider transport – if you'll be flying with the bike, think about getting S & S couplers so you can break it into smaller segments.

Single bikes: As your child gets older, a single bike of her own becomes an option. You will have to consider all aspects of your child before making the decision to put her on her own bike – physical strength, coordination, ability to be aware of surroundings, experience in traffic, and maturity.

If your child can handle her own bike, it can lead to a greater sense of independence and satisfaction; if she can't it can lead to disaster.

Family Examples

Each family is unique and will make a decision based on their strengths, weaknesses, personalities, and experiences. Here are a few families who have toured extensively and how/why they made the choice they did.

The Vogel Family - Our first tentative forays into the bike touring world with children came on tandems. John and I had toured extensively before our boys were born and knew we wanted to tour with them. When the boys were 7 we bought a couple of tandems and hit the road for short 2- or 4-day tours. It quickly became apparent there was a problem with the picture.

John is a much stronger cyclist than I am and he goes much faster then me. The child on his bike reached a nice break spot and got off the bike to play. He played and played and played – and then I showed up with my kid and John was ready to take off again. It didn't take long before both boys refused to ride on my bike. I can't say I blamed them – who would want to ride with a slowpoke?

When we considered taking off for a year-long tour when the boys were eight, we knew we couldn't use our tandems – nobody would ride with me. At the time, the boys were not mature enough to handle their own bikes. We ended up with a triple bike for John and the boys while I rode behind them on my single. That combination was the perfect equalizer and I ended up being able to stay right with them most of the time – and occasionally I even went faster!

Although the triple/single combination worked perfectly for us at the time, there were several disadvantages to think about if you are considering this option:

- **Hard to get up hills** – John really struggled to get the triple uphill. Tandems are notoriously slow on hills, and a triple is even slower. The boys generally got off and walked up while John pedaled up solo.
- **Long & cumbersome** – the triple with BOB trailer was a whopping 14-feet long! Try getting that into hotel rooms or on ferries or through tight city streets!
- **Difficult to handle** – The triple required an enormous amount of upper body strength and it took John quite a while to build up the strength to handle it. In the meantime, he was perpetually sore. Also, every movement of any rider is magnified, so controlling the bike with two wiggly children was a challenge.
- **I was left out** – John and the boys were together all the time and developed a very tight relationship. Although I was near them all the time, I wasn't privy to their private conversations on the bike and, at times, felt left out.
- **The boys were always together** – siblings tend to fight at times, and ours are no exception. Given the fact that they were right together, joined at the hip so to speak, they sometimes got on each other's nerves and couldn't get away. When they started fighting on the bike, they threw the balance off so that it was hard for John to control it.

When we decided to head out to **cycle the Pan American Highway from Alaska to Argentina** a couple years later, we again went back to that basic decision – what kind of bikes should we take? By that point, our boys had already cycled a lot and knew exactly what to expect. When we asked them what they wanted, Davy immediately said he wanted a single; Daryl voted for a tandem.

John and I were leaning toward two tandems – we weren't sure Davy could handle a single for 17,000 miles through 15 countries. We felt safer with our sons on our bikes so we could control them – we trusted our own abilities more than the boys'. However, we decided to allow the boys to make the decision and bought a tandem for John and Daryl, and singles for me and Davy. It was the perfect decision!

At first, Davy did not have the skills necessary to maneuver through heavy traffic. When we hit a city, we sandwiched him between us so he could see the example of the parent in front, while the one behind was there to scream at him to get back over if he started to make a mistake. He felt very safe and secure, and tackled cities with no fear whatsoever.

By the time he turned 11 Davy had 6000 miles under his belt and was perfectly capable of getting himself through whatever conditions he found himself in. He had the physical strength to take the bike up steep Andean mountains and the presence of mind to know exactly what was going on around him at all times.

His twin brother, however, could never ride a single bike on tour at that age. Daryl simply didn't have the physical strength or coordination he would need to successfully handle his own bike. He tended to daydream, and would not be aware of traffic conditions around him. Putting him on his own bike would have been tantamount to murder – he simply was not mature enough physically, mentally or emotionally to handle the demands.

The Verhage Family – We set out from Los Angeles, California heading south toward South America with our two boys (aged 10 and 12) on two tandems. Although both Jesse and Sammy were very capable riders, all four members of our family felt more secure on the tandems rather than having the boys on their own bikes.

We felt more confident having the boys on our bikes rather than on bikes of their own for safety reasons. Besides that, we liked the fact that we could carry on a conversation while riding which brought us closer together.

As the boys grew older, they wanted more independence. We ended up putting the two adults on tandem and the two boys on the other.

The disadvantage to the tandems is primarily a transportation issue – when we want to hitch we have to find a vehicle big enough to take both tandems. We have managed to hitch a lot, so I guess it can't be too much of a hassle!

The Williams Family - Our decision to tour on a triple came after finding a Santana Triple on Craig's List and contacting other families to get their input on what it was like to tour on a triple. We drove from Northern California to Lake Tahoe one snowy day, rode the bike (on freshly plowed streets no less) and instantly decided this bike was for us.

The biggest plus for us was that the bike is a great equalizer. I am not as strong a cyclist as Mike and on our 1994 cross-country tour on single bikes he was always waiting at the top of each climb, cooled down and ready to go, when I arrived. It was important to us that we could be together as a family so we could share the experiences of the road as we came across them.

Another huge plus was that our child was with us on the bike and we didn't have to worry about him being separated from us. His safety was more or less ensured being with us and our worries were lessened.

Overall communication on the triple worked out fine however the middle person (in this case me, Mom) often had to relay information from either end to the other.

At first I wasn't sure I'd like my 9-year old son in the third position because I couldn't see him in full view but I actually liked this configuration. I could peek at him with the rear view mirror but he also had a bit of "privacy" and I could listen to him as he made up stories and had his own little adventures as we pedaled along. He liked being on the back and could stand on the uphill to give us a boost. He earned the nicknames, "Turbo," "Afterburner," and "Accelerator."

Disadvantages of a Triple:

- **Climbing** — When climbing steep grades the front two positions must sit and grind in the lowest gear. Our son could stand and provide extra power but all three riders standing was out of the question. When we first started out we couldn't even ride a 7 percent grade but eventually we could by picking a post or guardrail to ride to and catch our breath before moving on. We were finally able to ride a 17 percent grade without stopping so it does get easier! Steep hills are a killer though!
- **Control** — The triple requires a lot of upper body strength and control from the captain. The bike can be difficult to control with the weight of three riders and gear. (We figured our bike weighed about 75 lbs including racks, fenders, bottle cages, etc.; the panniers, BOB trailer and gear were about another 150 lbs. and our body weight was about 400 lbs. for a grand total of 625 whopping lbs.) Mike said that getting the weight in the panniers evenly distributed was key and he got stronger as we went along. As a team we had to learn to be "body quiet" on the bike. That means no jerking motions or leaning because this would have a huge impact on Mike's ability to control the bike.
- **Braking** — A lot of newer triples and tandems are using disc brakes (front and back) which requires constant use of the brake levers on the downhill causing soreness in the hands on long descents. We preferred a drum brake on the rear that works on a separate thumb shifter that can be used as a drag to slow the bike down minimizing the use of the hand brakes. (Drum brakes are heavy but we felt it was a good trade off when you have a lot of steep descents.)
- **Gears** — Because the captain can't see what gear he is in he has to count on the rear stoker to tell him the gearing or he needs a computer that indicates the gearing such as the Shimano Flight. Also, on a triple the captain can't hear if the chain is rubbing on the front derailleur. Gregory and I were constantly telling Mike to adjust.
- **Tires** — You go through tires quickly due to running a higher psi and having extra weight. We ran Continental Ultra Gatorskins 700x28 at 145psi and went through 5 sets in about

4,000 miles. (Santana recommended these tires and pressure with replacement at every 800-1,000 miles.)

- **Wheels** — The rear wheel is under more stress with three people therefore a greater chance of broken spokes exists.
- **Illness** — If one (or heaven forbid two) riders are having a bad day it requires the others to take up the slack and this is especially tough if you are doing a lot of climbing or fighting headwinds. I remember one day when Mike's knee was especially hurting and I had to take up the slack. I was completely exhausted at the end of the day and praying for his quick recovery! You definitely need 100 percent effort from everyone to have the optimum experience. This includes being mentally in the game as well. Some days it is mind over matter and you have to all be able to tell yourselves that you can do it!

Even given the above disadvantages I have to say that we love our triple. It has brought our family closer together having shared this experience of touring across America. Joys and heartaches are intensified but you learn to quickly overcome tough situations because you must to prevail in this endeavor. The triple also opens you up to meeting the most kind and generous people who are enamored with what you are doing and want to share in your unique adventure. The triple and our tour are certainly one of the best gifts we have given to our son and ourselves.

Feldmann family: Honestly, we never even considered anything other than singles for all four of us. Our boys (aged 9 and 12) were very confident on their bikes and we all knew they could ride across Canada on their own.

<u>The Tomlinson Family</u>: The reason we chose a tandem was that Kate, aged 8 at the time, was too big to go in a trailer but still not strong enough to cycle the daily mileage on her own bike. She rides as a stoker behind my husband while I ride a single alongside them. A tandem was the obvious choice as this way she feels very much part of the team - a participant rather than just a passenger so she is feeling a sense of achievement. My husband reckons she is at least carrying her own weight.

<u>The Miller Family:</u> When we took off in 2008 to cycle across Europe and into North Africa our four kids were ages 5-11. We spent a lot of time trying to figure out what would work best for our family and the kids' various sizes and abilities. What we ended up with were REI Novara touring bikes for my husband and me with Adams Trail-A-Bikes attached to those for the younger two boys, ages five and seven. We got regular kids bikes for our two older children which we spent about $200 each upgrading components on.

My husband, Tony, built a custom rack for the Adams Trail-A-Bike that accommodated one of our roll bags. When we rode, Tony and his little person went first, our older two children rode in the middle and I brought up the rear with my little person.

We were happy with the Trail-A-Bikes because they allowed us to disconnect the kids' bikes when we were boarding ferries or trains. They were also nice if we needed to run into town, one or the other of us, to do some shopping.

Chapter 4: Packing and Preparation

It's time to put it all together and actually get that gear on the bike. But what to pack?

Most people tend to pack too much – you really need very little! The most important thing to consider is to make sure everything you take fits and is comfortable – there is nothing worse than spending all day pedaling while uncomfortable.

While each person packs slightly different, here is our packing list – everything we needed for the four of us. This is a complete list of the gear and equipment we carried on our bicycles. It includes items for two adults along with two 12-year old boys who were being roadschooled.

You will need to tweek this list depending on your circumstances. We carried gear and equipment for all four seasons since we encountered it all – you may very well be able to eliminate some of this. We also traveled in countries with little in the way of bicycle support, so needed to carry more replacements and tools than you will most likely need.

CAMPING:
- Tent – we started with a 4-person tent, but switched to two 2-person tents after a couple of years. Get what feels right to you.
- Sleeping Bags
- Foam/Air Mattresses
- Pillows
- Flashlights - We believe it's important to have a flashlight for each of us since we all do a lot of reading and the kids were

being homeschooled. This was more important during the winter when we spent a lot of time in the tent due to short days.

- Tarp (large) - Large enough to cover the bikes in a rainstorm. There were times when we were caught in a heavy rainstorm and our only protection was making an impromptu tent with us straddling our bikes with the tarp covering us! The tarp had multiple uses including theft protection by covering the bikes with it at night.

EATING/COOKING:
- Stove
- Bowls (4)
- Utensils - spoons(4), forks(4), knives(2)
- Serrated cutting knife (a regular one. We wrapped it in plastic bags to prevent cutting panniers)
- Big wooden spoon
- Pot (we carried a 4-liter pot so we could make pasta for four)
- Lighter
- Spare parts for the stove
- Spare fuel bottle
- Hot pads for holding pot
- Iodine drops to purify water
- Food (the amount and kind varied tremendously depending on where we were and how far we had to go before we could buy more. We always had something like granola bars or other snacks with us.)

CLOTHING:
1. **Bicycle Clothing:**
   - Bicycle helmets
   - T-shirts, bicycling shorts, regular shorts, socks - about two apiece. I also had 2 sports bras. (We wore regular shorts over our bicycle shorts and regular cotton t-shirts)
   - Shoes – John used cleated cycling shoes while the rest of us used regular sneakers with toe clips or Power Grips

- Sweat bands - Critical when climbing long, steep hills in the tropics. (Need to be thin enough to comfortably fit under helmet. We used Head Sweats)
- Bicycling gloves

2. Off-Bike Clothing:
- Sandals for each of us
- Sneakers (John)
- Sweat pants or long pants
- Skirt (me only)
- Cap/visor

3. Winter Clothing:
- Hats - A thin wool hat to wear under the helmet
- Gloves - Winter gloves; wool works best
- Liner Gloves - To insert inside the winter gloves; wool works best
- Neck gaiters - John didn't cover his face, but the boys and I liked to cover our noses and mouths when cold.
- Long Sleeve Shirts - thin wool and thin cotton shirts to use in layers
- Felted wool sweater vests - Daryl and I tended to get cold easily so needed an extra layer
- Jackets - either down jackets or thick felted wool sweater
- Raincoats/rainpants - To use for warmth (they act to stop the cold wind from penetrating into our layers of shirts) and to keep out moisture.
- Tights - the boys had two pairs each to layer; wool works best as it insulates even when wet
- Wool socks - a thin pair and a thick pair for each of us

BICYCLES:
- Bicycles with racks
- Panniers (saddle bags) and Trailers - A full set of panniers (front, rear, and handlebar) for all bikes plus two trailers.
- Dry bags – for sleeping bags and pads and other bulky items. These were strapped on top of the trailers or on our rear racks.

- Spare tubes - More 700c tubes than 26" since the former were very difficult (if not impossible) to get in South or Central America. A spare tube for the trailer.
- Spare tires - Again more 700c tires for the same reason. A spare tire for the trailer.
- Flat Tire Kit (patch kit, 3 plastic tire spoons, spare tube) for two adult bikes.
- Pumps - One on each bike
- Emergency Flashing Lights - For when we got caught in the dark or went through tunnels
- Water bottles
- Pressure gauge
- Chain lube
- Cable lock
- Cycle computer
- Nylon webbing straps/bungee cords to hold things together and on to racks
- Extra side-release fastener for the nylon webbing straps
- Tool kit
- Spare chain links
- Dedicated 10mm wrench
- Dedicated 8 mm wrench
- Small adjustable wrench
- Dedicated allen wrenches
- Small pliers
- Various nuts, bolts, and spacers
- Spare chain
- Spare freewheel
- Dedicated spoke wrench
- Freewheel removal tool
- Chain whip (to remove the freewheel with)
- Dedicated chain breaker
- Crank remover
- Spare brake and shifter cables
- Valve cap which doubled as a tool to remove Schrader valve
- Multi-tool: Allen wrenches, screw drivers, star tool, chain breaker
- Spare cantilever and disk brake pads

- Presta to Schrader valve converter
- Timing chain adjuster (for tandem)

ROADSCHOOLING:
- Journals - small spiral notebooks. We sent them home when filled.
- Math books - a book for each kid at their level.
- Kindles – each kid had one and we downloaded books from Amazon.com
- Pencil bag - filled with pens, pencils, pencil sharpener, erasers, compass, protractor, and ruler
- Sketchpad
- Colored pencils
- Computer software - Various math and language arts programs
- Spanish dictionary
- Calculator

TECHNICAL:
- Laptop computers (2)
- Sony camera
- Spare lithium ion battery for Sony camera
- Cannon video camera
- Flip video camera
- AA battery charger
- Rechargeable AA batteries
- External microphone (for Skype and recording on the computer)
- SDHC memory cards (3)
- Flash memory drives(3)
- Camera to USB cable
- Mini tripod
- Point-and-Click camera
- Blank DVD's
- External CD/DVD reader/writer
- USB mice (2)
- Spare software (Photoshop, MS Word, and Pinnacle Studio Plus)

- Large freezer bags (when needed to protect computers)

TOILETRIES & MEDICAL:
- Antibiotic ointment
- Ibuprofen
- Paper tape
- Gauze
- Band-Aids
- Antihistamine ointment
- Anti-inflammant cream
- Q-tips
- Lice comb
- Allergy medicine
- Throat lozenges
- Toothbrushes
- Toothpaste
- Dental floss
- Shampoo
- Wet Ones
- Deodorant
- Chapstick with sunscreen
- Prescription drugs
- Multi-vitamins
- Toilet paper - an essential!
- Bug spray
- Sunscreen

MISCELANEOUS:
- Beads – I am a bead artist, so I carried a small pack with an assortment of beads, thread, and needles. This doubled as a mending kit.
- Extra batteries
- mP3 player/headphones
- Eyeglass lens cleaner/cloth
- Sunglasses (prescription for Davy & John)
- Nintendo DS handheld game
- Leatherman w/ pliers

- Pacsafe money belt
- Extra plastic bags (for when we got caught in a rain storm)
- Compact, foldable day pack
- Checkbook (in case we needed to send in a payment)
- Duct tape
- Electrical tape
- Extra shoelaces
- Playing Cards/Dice
- Driver's License (parents)
- Passports

Chapter 5: Tips for Touring with Kids

You're all packed up and ready to hit the road. Now what?

First of all, don't panic. Everything will be OK – I promise! Yes, you'll make mistakes. Yes, you'll come back home with a list a mile long of things you'll do differently next time. That's OK – the important thing is to have fun and learn from your mistakes!

Shorten your distances: while you may be comfortable with 100-mile days, your child most likely won't be. As adults, it can be hard for us to accept a 20-mile day when we're used to a minimum of 50. But really – what's the rush? Take time to enjoy that 20 miles and spread it out throughout the day.

Take lots of breaks: While the time spent pedaling may very well be the highlight of your tour, your child will most likely remember the breaks. Take breaks frequently and play with your children. Watch ants milling about their pile, throw stones into a stream, or use a guard rail as a balance beam. Look around and be creative during your breaks and your kids will be off and running the second they get off the bike! We take hour-long breaks frequently throughout the day, and enjoy them playing and interacting with the kids – throwing rocks into water, hiking to a waterfall, playing baseball with pinecones and sticks, or playing soccer with an old soda bottle. When the kids look back on the trip, they generally remember these times, not riding.

Eat a lot: Plan on pulling out food at each break. Kids tend to burn off energy much faster than adults and will need to eat more frequently. A full belly leads to a happy kid. Food with a higher fat content will stay with her longer than pure carbs – mix nuts with the dried fruit, eat some cheese or peanut butter with the apple, or stop for ice cream!

Drink: Children tend to forget to drink, so you'll have to remind your child repeatedly to drink water. Don't let him get dehydrated! Plain water is fine for most circumstances, but if you are sweating profusely, consider Gatorade or something similar to replace the electrolytes you're sweating out.

Celebrate success: Nothing drives kids on like success. Celebrate anything and everything – cresting the top of the hill, making it seven kilometers without a break, crossing a state border… No success is too small for a celebration! A high five, a group hug, or a chocolate bar is all you need to let your little one know you are proud of her.

Never doubt your child
Never, ever doubt your child
Remember that kids are capable of lots more than you think
Keep kids in the loop
Make sure bike and clothes fit properly
Keep snacks in cut-off water bottle on handlebar
Have kids help with decisions
Study the map with kids
Get plenty of sleep
Take advantage of cool hours when hot
Take advantage of warmer times when cold
When you have a tailwind - ride fast and far
Don't ride against a headwind - it'll only wear you out
Let kids take as many toys as they can cram into their personal space
Take lots of days off
Take time to smell the roses
Learn something in every single place you go
Eat local food
Encourage the kids to play with local children
Carry layers, layers, and more layers
Play games during breaks
Have smaller, weaker children on tandem
Take advantage of cultural events where ever you are
Pack equipment in waterproof bags
Stop at the city park so the kids can slide down the slide
Pack wool clothes if you'll be in cold temps
Plan lots of time off the bikes
Ask permission to set up your tent in unusual places
Give your child lots and lots of hugs
Choose roads with wide shoulders
Trust your kids – they know more than you think
Tell them you love them
Let kids lead so they feel more in control
Look for kid-friendly destinations
If you find a water park, stop (even if you've only pedaled three miles)
Keep your child's bike as light as possible
Stop at any place that looks interesting
Sleep out under the stars regularly
Stop for ice cream!

Chapter 6: Where to Sleep at Night

One of the first questions people ask us is, "Where do you sleep at night?" It's an uncomforting thought to think of being stranded on the side of the road with your children. We've found, in our years on the road, that **we always manage to find a safe spot to sleep**. Always. It might not be ideal, but we've never ended up stranded.

People throughout the world have three basic needs – food, water, and a place to sleep. If you find yourselves without a place for the night, don't be afraid to reach out to others for help – they'll most likely be more than happy to help.

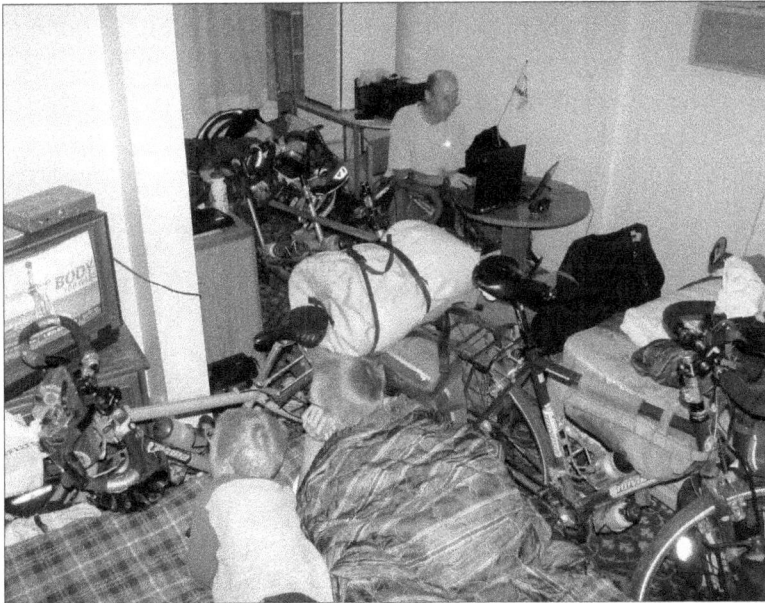

Hotels: Depending on your budget, you may end up staying in hotels on a fairly regular basis. In some countries they are more expensive than others and you might go through phases. We camped almost exclusively throughout Canada and the US, but started staying in hotels in Central America where they were within our price range. There are times, however, when the next hotel is too far for us to reach in a day. You will need some backup in case you can't find a hotel.

Campgrounds:
Campgrounds are great if you can find them. In some areas – like the Pacific Coast, for example – you'll find nice campgrounds every night. In other areas, they simply don't exist. Some RV parks allow tents, others do not. Campgrounds are nice, safe places and generally have showers and picnic tables available, but don't rely on finding them every night. If you are traveling in high season, it would be a good idea to make reservations as they tend to fill up. Some state parks will always find space for a bike tourist – they have a regulation to never turn away anyone traveling on a bike.

Warmshowers:
Warmshowers.org is a great resource for bicycle tourists of all ages. It is a hospitality site designed specifically for bike tourists. This is a great resource for places to stay in cities, but not so great for small towns as most of the hosts tend to live in cities. Be sure to write in advance and communicate well with your host so they know when you'll be arriving.

Wild Camping: This is where you get creative. The idea here is to pull off the road and find a spot in the woods where nobody even knows you are there. Never pull in to an area marked "No Trespassing", do not have a fire, and leave no trace. When it is nearly dark, wait until no cars are coming before quickly heading into the woods. It takes some practice to find good wild camping spots, but after a while you will be able to find a spot nearly anywhere you look.

Ask permission: We frequently ask permission to camp in people's yards or behind a restaurant or in a church yard. We've met some wonderful people this way! People are nearly always willing to help you out and will sometimes even invite you into their homes.

Chapter 7: What to Eat

Food is basic to our survival, and on tour your life will start to revolve around food very quickly. **You will be demanding a lot of your body and will need to provide it with quality food in order for it to perform at its peak.**

Since you'll be on the go all day, you'll need more calories than you needed at home. For the first month or so on the bike, your body will be trying to adapt and will require a lot of food. After a while, you'll find two things happening:

- **you'll figure out what kinds of foods and how much works for you**
- **your body will adapt to the demands of bike touring and you won't need as much**

For your kids, however, that adaptation period will take longer. At first, plan on pulling out food at every break. You won't need a lot – a handful of dried fruit and nuts, a granola bar, or fresh broccoli with dip. You'll quickly discover how your child's energy level is directly proportional to the amount of food he eats.

One tip that might help your child consume enough calories is to **mount a cut-off water bottle on your child's handlebars.** You can fill the cup with nuts or other snacks and he can snack while you are riding.

Snacks are what you'll be pulling out throughout the day. They need to be easily accessible and quick to eat. Here's a list of snack foods we frequently carried. Look around your grocery store and pick up whatever looks good.

- Dried fruit and nuts
- Apples (sometimes we smear peanut butter on them)

- Granola bars (these come in an incredible array of varieties in the USA)
- Crackers and cheese
- Fresh broccoli with dip
- Baby carrots
- Beef jerky
- Yogurt (need to eat it at the first break)

For your main meals, you'll have to decide if you want to carry a stove (and accompanying pot, spoon, fuel, etc...) or if you'll eat in restaurants. It's a personal decision and there is no right and wrong. We cooked almost exclusively throughout the USA and Canada, but rarely pulled out the stove in Central America.

Remember, if you plan to cook your own meals, you'll need to make sure you have a water source for both cooking and cleaning up. That's easy to do if you are in a campground or near a river, but difficult if you are in the desert. It's hard to carry enough water for drinking, cooking, and cleaning.

For food for cooking, the side dish aisle of the supermarket will be your best friend. We've found we typically need one entire package of Rice-a-Roni each as our dinner. You can add canned tuna or other canned meat and some chopped veggies to any of the packaged side dishes to make them into a hearty, filling meal.

- Rice-a-Roni (lots of different varieties here!)
- Instant mashed potatoes
- Pasta - either one of the mixes with sauce included or buy plain pasta and a jar of sauce
- Soup mixes – we like to add some sausage or other meat
- Fresh potatoes – we prefer real potatoes over instant so will cook them whenever we are able.
- Veggies – broccoli is easy to carry and cooks easily, but nearly any vegetable works. Simply cook them in the pot with the pasta or rice.

Chapter 8: Benefits of Touring for Children

Exercise: in today's society where children typically less than 30 minutes per day of exercise, a bike tour is great for getting kids active. In addition to the exercise he will be getting while on tour itself, he'll be learning that being active simply feels good – therefore he'll be more likely to remain active once back home.

Education: one of the things we teachers discovered ages ago was that kids learn best if they are actively involved and are learning more than one sense. Reading about something is one thing, but seeing, feeling, hearing, smelling, and touching it makes it come alive. As you tour on your bike, you will come across many, many opportunities to learn. Take advantage of roadside historical signs, visit state and national parks, and discuss the intricacies of tree and flower design during breaks,

Time with parents: Too many kids are growing up with very little interaction with their parents as it becomes more necessary to work longer hours just to survive. Once you are on the road, you'll

41

leave work behind and have time with your children. Quality, one-on-one, uninterrupted time. They say time is the best gift a parent can give their child; a bike tour will give you that time.

Unplugged: The average child in the US today spends seven hours each day in front of the TV or computer. Getting him away from the computer will allow him to develop other creative skills he can only get by being outdoors in Mother Nature's handiwork.

Chapter 9: Special Considerations for an Extended Tour

Many of us dream of taking off to travel the world for extended periods of time. One of the things we've learned is that a long-term bike tour with your children is more accessible than you might think. Surprisingly, the preparation for the biking itself is no more than planning for a month-long tour. It's the stuff involved with putting your life on hold for years that takes time.

What about school, you might ask. How will my children learn all they need to know if we take off on our bikes? Or what about my job? Or the million other demands placed upon me? You may feel locked in by the demands and expectations of society. You feel you have to hold a steady job and work from 9 – 5; the kids need to go to school and play on the soccer team. That's what is expected of you – that's what you "should" do.

When it comes right down to it, there are many ways to raise a child and no one of them is "right". They are simply different. Research indicates that kids who are raised in a stimulating environment and are encouraged to explore and discover learn at a faster rate and in more depth. They are able to create connections more readily and develop a deeper understanding of the world around them. A bike tour provides all of that.

You don't have to put your dreams of traveling on bicycle off until your children have left the house. Living your dream with children is a rewarding, exhilarating experience, and will build unforgettable memories for both you and your child.

Children have an amazing capacity for picking up on their parents' passions and becoming passionate about them themselves. If Mom and Dad are committed to living aboard a sailboat, their kids will wholeheartedly embrace the idea. If parents are excited about an extended backpacking trip, their kids will be too. If Mom and Dad are committed to riding their bikes around the world, the kids will be thrilled as well.

But then you come back to: "Where do I even start?" All I can say is to simply make the decision to do it, announce it to your friends and family, and then put one foot in front of the other.

I remember so clearly that whirlwind of activity before we could hit the road for our multi-year Pan American ride. The journey itself would be the easy part – get on the bikes and ride. But the background preparation threatened to overtake us and derail the project before we even got on the road. Our to-do list grew longer by the day, and I wondered if it would ever get done before departure day arrived.

We needed to remodel the house for renters, dismantle the boys' treehouse, create a website and look for sponsors, research how to manage and access our money from remote corners of the world. Figure out how to ship the bikes and gear to the northern end of the world. Get everything we owned sorted into three piles – "sell," "store," or "take with."

And all the time, we tried to maintain some sense of normality. The boys attended fourth grade at a local elementary school and played on soccer teams. They took swim lessons at the YMCA and Daryl joined the swim team. I headed out to a local high school every morning, where I taught Special Education classes. John became our stay-at-home dad and tried to keep things together at the same time as we dismantled our lives.

But slowly, day by day, our departure grew nearer. Things got checked off that list. And somehow, miraculously, our lives had been reduced down to eight boxes in our driveway by the time our plane was scheduled to leave.

If we could do it, you can too. You'll probably come up with many more items for this list, but this will give you a good start for your planning.

Your house: Some families make the decision to sell their house so they are free and unencumbered. Others choose to rent it out. Consider your circumstances and make the decision that's right for you.

We opted to keep our house and rent it out. The house was paid for, and the rent income paid about half of our monthly expenses. Besides that, we have a barn behind our house, so we stored our belongings there and didn't have to pay a storage locker. We hired a property management firm that came highly recommended by a friend. It was well worth the monthly fee in order to not have to hassle with the house at all.

Consider:
- How much are your payments? Would the rent you could charge cover them?
- Is your house where you ultimately want to live? Could this be an opportunity to relocate?
- Is there any kind of sentimental attachment to the house?

Your belongings: What will you do with all your stuff? Some families decide to get rid of nearly everything and only leave a box or two with parents or siblings, while others decide to pack it all away. We happen to have a barn behind our house, so opted to store a lot – that way we wouldn't have to replace it when we got back home and we weren't paying anything to store it.

Consider:
- Do you have a place to store stuff, or would you be renting a storage locker? Would it be cheaper to store it, or replace it once you get back home?
- How much sentimental value does it have? If there is something that is very precious to you, it will most likely be worth it to store it, even if it costs more.

Roadschooling: Check the regulations for your state or country. In Idaho, where we are from, there are no guidelines at all – we only had to tell the boys' local school we would be homeschooling the boys. In some states or countries, you will have to provide detailed documentation about what you are doing with your child.

Consider:
- Do you feel comfortable using your journey as the base for your educational program? Or would a published series be a better choice for you?
- Are your children self-motivated? Or will you need to provide most of the guidance?
- It may be worth it to change your official residence to a state with fewer regulations.

Finances: Getting our finances organized was one of the biggest hassles we faced when preparing to take off for nearly three years. Be aware that mail stops will be few and far between, so don't rely on getting mail on a regular basis.

Consider:
- A forwarding order at the post office is only good for six months, so be sure to change all addresses to someone who can deal with it for you.
- In the US (and I assume in other countries as well) there are mail forwarding services who will hold your mail until you send them an address. If you don't have someone who will help you out, sign up with one of these services.
- Get all bills set up for online payment.

- Set up online banking for all bank accounts.
- Open a Schwab One account or an account at Capital One Bank so you won't have to pay ATM fees anywhere in the world.
- Get a small amount of travelers checks as backup, but you will most likely be able to get all money needed from ATMs.
- Email all credit card numbers and their phone numbers to yourself. If something happens, you can generally always find email access to get the information. Be sure to photocopy everything and have it with you as well.

Health: Health is a very real consideration on a long tour. An accident or sickness can easily be the end of the journey, and could very well have long-term ramifications.

Consider:

- Get health insurance. You may be able to continue your current policy, but check into it carefully. Many policies will only continue for a certain amount of time after you've left your job or they will only cover you in certain locations around the world. We picked up a policy from IMG that is designed for expats and long-term travelers. We could only get it once we were out of the USA and have to be outside the country for at least six months every year, but we are covered in case we have a major accident or long-term sickness.
- Be sure to eat a good variety of foods, including plenty of fruits and vegetables. There will be plenty of times when fresh food is more expensive and it's easy to decide to go without in order to save money. Don't do it! Your body needs the vitamins and minerals it can only get from fresh foods.
- Set your pace. If you are out for only a few months, you'll be able to push your body hard the whole time. However, on a long tour, you will need to carefully consider a pace you can maintain for months on end. Don't wear yourself out!

Gear and Equipment: If you are considering an extended tour, you'll need to make sure your gear and equipment is up to the challenge. For a short tour with an easy out if your equipment fails, you can get by with cheaper equipment. But for the long-term, quality gear is essential and will be cheaper in the long run.

Consider:

- You'll most like spend quite a few nights in your tent. Get heavy duty flooring as the ground surface will frequently be rough. Be sure your tent can handle fairly high winds in case you get caught unawares and need to stop in less-than-ideal conditions.
- What about a stove and pots? Will you depend on restaurants or cook your own? What kind of stove do you need – butane cartridges are convenient, but can be hard to find. Gas is messy, but hot. Alcohol is clean, but may be hard to find.

- Get good quality panniers that will hold together. If you pay more for them now, they'll last you many, many years. One set of panniers we are using on our Pan American journey was old and well used when I met John 20 years ago – and it is still going strong!
- Don't skimp on racks! You'll need good, solid, heavy-duty racks in order to carry all the gear you'll need without breaking.
- Consider the conditions and pack accordingly. If you'll be out for extended periods of time, chances are you'll encounter all kinds of weather conditions. You'll need clothes for both heat and cold and sleeping bags that can deal with the coldest temps you'll pass through.

Bike Maintenance: Be sure you can do most repairs to your bike on your own. Depending on where you will be touring, you may or may not have access to bike shops that can help you out.

Consider:
- If you aren't comfortable with bike maintenance, you might want to take a class to learn the basics. You don't want to get caught out in the middle of nowhere with no way to repair your bike!

Extended travel with your children is a fabulous experience for all involved. Although it may seem like an impossible task to get ready, you'll be glad you did it in the end! I hope I've answered a few of those millions of questions swirling around in your mind. We've got an extensive resource section on our website (www.familyonbikes.org) that will answer many more questions. If you have others, I would be happy to do my best to help you out – write to me at familyonbikes@gmail.com

www.ingramcontent.com/pod-product-compliance
Lightning Source LLC
Chambersburg PA
CBHW060618030426
42337CB00018B/3110